Y0-ATD-018

A COMMON of PISCARY

To Ken and Jan
affectionately

Ben.

A COMMON
of
PISCARY

&

OTHER POEMS

by

Ben Wolf

with illustrations by the author

SUTTER HOUSE

1981

AUTHOR'S NOTE

The drawings appearing with these verses are not necessarily to be considered illustrations for specific poems; rather, they are akin in spirit and intended solely as visual enhancement.

Copyright © 1981 by Ben Wolf

All rights reserved

LIBRARY OF CONGRESS CATALOGING IN PUBLICATION DATA

Wolf, Ben.
  A common of piscary & other poems.

  I. Title.
PS3573.0476C6   811'.54   81-14605
ISBN 0-915010-32-1   AACR2

SUTTER HOUSE
LITITZ, PENNSYLVANIA 17543

PRINTED IN THE UNITED STATES OF AMERICA

FOREWORD

As one of those who insisted that the author of these poems publish them, I'm quite content right now. Here they are.

Something that was worth doing is at this moment where it should be: in bookshops, available at last to everyone with a taste for poetry.

Ben Wolf's diffidence has hitherto kept his verse within a limited circle of readers, but those readers have long wanted to share their good fortune with others.

The considerable public that already knows Ben Wolf as painter, print-maker, caricaturist, art critic, and biographer will, I feel sure, welcome his poetry too.

It is verse that respects both itself and the reader: no verbal or typographic gimmicks, no pseudo-metaphysical mush, no esoteric mumbling, no straining for effect whatever. Here is a poet quietly at work, very quietly; yet somehow in these pages we can hear the pounding surf of his beloved sea—and even "the roistering birds of youth."

Again and again we come upon a beautifully evocative line, or a line positively purring with wit, or a line illuminating some age-old mystery. And they stick in the memory.

SEYMOUR ADELMAN

For Ruth

I would sit with those
At sundown
Who stood fast friends
At noon.

I shall lie next you
At nightfall
Who walked with me
All day.

I

A Common of Piscary

Beyond the rights of land and law
Beneath the marbled main,
Vast treasures tempt the poet's skill
To net a deathless line.

Five fathoms deep where Shakespeare plumbed,
Where brooded Ahab's whale
And died the pinioned Albatross
Upon a painted sea,
There fatuous rhymesters test their luck
Against the weight of time,
For though they drown amid their words
Recruits shall ever strive.

Pis'cary:—1. *Law.* The right or privilege of fishing in another
man's waters;—now in phrase *common of piscary*.

WEBSTER'S DICTIONARY

II

Dry locust limbs scrape loose
The silverfish
Beneath the roof-breasts
Of the widow's walk . . .

Scratching shingled memories . . .
Death-clutching dreams . . .
That flit
Like Elmo's Fire along
The wind-flung clapboard ribs
Now caved upon
A tideless tor of weed.

Until
The last boards dip beneath
The brackish marsh . . .
Beyond the cloud-high ken
Of diving birds . . .
The sea bride
Sunken in her hollow hull
Will keen a curling dirge
Against the harping fingers of the waves
For lovers lost
Within the dust-deep mist.

III

I stroll upon the vast seaverge
To watch
The daily commerce
Of the tides.

I tread the rocky castaways
Strewn and tumbled by the seas
And . . . while I witness . . .
Feel my transience.

Old and hoar
This kelp-wrapped ritual
Upon that time-eroded day
Some primal venturer
Crept ashore
To risk
The unfamiliar air.

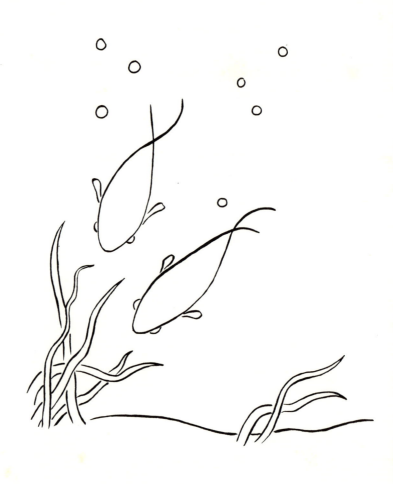

IV

Little fishes
Of the sea . . .
You cannot stride
The earth — like me!

Prideful plodder
Of the land,
Can you swim
A saraband?

V

Pull the waves together
With a spidery hairnet
And hold within its grasp
Ideas . . .
Teeming life . . .
A sargasso of regrets
And little fishes
Well preservèd
In remorseful brine.

VI

I saw two monsters
Fighting in the sea . . .
Ebb-tide bared boots . . .
Where lies reality?

VII

Seagulls soar
The opaque water plain.
Seek they survivors
Of their dreams in vain?

VIII

Pilings

Watercarved silhouettes
Beneath the stretching pier . . .
Rough-hewn spaces lurk
Between their forms.
They stand
Upon a tidal shrine . . .
Barnacled votives
Left by strayers to a sea-girt isle.

IX

Beyond the shallow reach of man
Vast grey Balaena sings . . .
Does Archean song perhaps recall
The Earth once trod upon
Before profound of Thalassa
An errant tribe reclaimed?

X

In the brine-dew
Of your eyes
I taste the plankton
Of some long-lost sea.

XI

When tide is out . . .
The litter is not made
Of bleaching sea-wrack
But of phantom friends.

XII

Sea dust . . .
Lacy mantle
On an ebony brow.

Sea dust . . .
Foam-child
Who wakes the nodding sea
Reminding it be restless.

Sea dust . . .
You waken destiny.

XIII

I made my love a diamond clasp
Of sunbeams from the sea
For her to wear within her heart
As long as memory.

XIV

Come . . .
Hear the stately converse
Of old trees
Where branches fin
The blue celestial seas.

Mark that quivering sapling
Fresh from birth . . .
Absorb the pungent dankness
Of wet earth.

Above a base
Of gnarled and knotted greaves
Regard the green mosaic
Of the leaves . . .

XV

A watercolorist is fog
Muting form with subtle brush
Smudging ships and sea and sky
Opaquing seabird's pivoting
Drowsing over all that's known,
A satin hushedness strange and far.

XVI

Pale grasses dance in grave ballet
Mated daisies nod a *pas de deux*
Birdcalls bend between wet boughs
Amorphous clouds laze by upon their backs.
One breathes the sea and wonders how
To meet the sense-numb night ahead.

XVII

This morning
At the old road's edge
Where such things
Tend to be
I saw a pale pink moth upon
A buttercup of gold.

Then
For elation's moment
Thrilled
In silent ecstasy
Until I turned
To vision share
And you
Were not beside.

XVIII

A russet leaf that fell
In nascent May
To daunt
The flaunted green of Spring
Now rasps unheard
Along the Summer lane
Beneath the roistering birds
Of youth.

XIX

It is recorded someplace
That opals be quite rare
Still I have seen them by the score
Upon the dew-hung fir.

They say to sing an aria
Takes years of arduous toil
Though I have heard the meadowlark
Who never works at all.

And while 'tis written elsewhere
That faith might mountains stir,
With greater ease the silent fog
Will make them disappear.

Man builds his great cathedrals
That seldom reach his God
Yet in the forest solitude
The trees do this each day.

XX

Great forest . . . shelter me.
Branches, nod your welcome here.
Birds be kind . . . sing assent
For I have left the city pall
And would be held by thee
Once more.

XXI

Butterflies

Although your span
Might shorter be
Than is the lot
Of grass and me . . .

Flitful petals
'Gainst the sky
At least you soar
Before you die.

XXII

I have never left
That lake
Where once
She waded deep . . .

For I have never touched
A sky as blue
Nor heard the leaves
Make music half so green.

XXIII

In Memoriam . . . Harry Kemp.

> While age-struck poet
> Pain-inched
> Down the street
>
> His child-soul
> Scamped before
> On scudding feet.

XXIV

A penny, sir?
The cost is high
For gossamer.

A penny, sir?
Occasion's rare
When magic lifts
The leaden lines.

A penny, sir?
For I must buy
A petaled rose
To die between
My loved one's breasts.

A penny, sir?
For I must lure
A lark
From innermost.

A penny, sir . . ?

XXV

A Drawing Is . . .

The echo of an unseen face
The shadow of a silent cry
An unformed thought
In a maze of half-wrought shapes.

A boneless whip . . .
An axe . . .
A moment
Woven in a clouded pool
By the wandering fingers
Of a dreaming child.

A knife-edged line
A feathered smudge
Beyond the knowing
Of its seed.

XXVI

Where shall I post
My pasquinade?
Upon what stone
Affix my bitter verse?

What bronze-eroding quip
To write . . .
What slashing thrust
At smug authority?

Upon the palace gate
There is a spot precise
That's quatrain-sized
Where all could clearly see!

But, ah, I am so rutted
Down my craven lane
That I shall stealth it
In my pocket's heart
Instead . . .

XXVII

Albion Spring

White petals thatch
The interlacing boughs
That shade
The verdant carpeting along
The curling Avon's bank.

Birdchoir joins
The ancient Abbey bells
To tell
*Another Spring
Has captured Bath!*

XXVIII

The man from Porlock
Came to pay a call
The Muses fled
But he remained to gall.

XXIX

For Nita Marquis Weil*

To stand upon the years
And not look down,
To find a flame
In each day's hearth
And turn from self
To give a spark away.

To count new faces
With the old,
To seek to learn
Fresh reasons why
And spendthrift beauty
After noon.

This is the triumph
You have made.

*On her eightieth birthday from B.W. on his
fiftieth. October 17th, 1964.

XXX

Nita . . . In Memoriam*

When she played hostess
To my mind
And met me in the antechamber
Of her thought,
I felt the probing
Of those age-blind eyes
That touched
My inner sightlessness . . .
Then I realized
That I mourned
Not her affliction
But my own.

*January 10th, 1974.

XXXI

Upon the ziggurats of mud
That lean against the sky
The priest must wait
For night's descent
To trace
The black-rimmed Braille.

But on the plain
The poet stands
To see stars blaze
At noon
Through stare-bleared eyes
That dare to read
Their runics
In the sun.

XXXII

They slammed the door
And took the key
To my inner ben
Of fantasy . . .

They think I'm barred
From dreams of art
But I shall pick
The lock apart!

XXXIII

Ovoid
Without end
The stretching
Generations reach . . .
A mystery wound
Within a coiling line.

XXXIV

Sick Child

Between the clutching sheets ensnared
Tight-tucked . . .
With mustard plaster on his chest
And starchy pillow
At his head . . .
The child hears voices muffling through
The louring window shades.

Youth shrills beyond the rooms
Rasping skate . . .
Batted ball . . .
Fugal wrangling from a sparrow's nest.

Beneath the chill white carapace
The child lies fettered in his bed
Yet dreams
Beyond the antiseptic womb.

XXXV

A Sherlockian Prayer

When I lay me down to sleep
I'd rather hear, while slumbering deep,
The dreamy strains of Sherlock's fiddle
Than solve the hissing Gollum's riddle.

Than quarterstaff with Robin's band
Or snatch black spot from Blind Pew's hand,
Than idle down a Romany road
Or venture motor trip with Toad,
Than sail the Alph to sunless sea
Or Dormouse join in cup of tea.

So if, dear Lord, you deem it meet
Just drop me off near Baker Street.

XXXVI

Pigeons on the beach
Like feathered hulls . . .
Can reproduce their kind
But never gulls.

XXXVII

A Time Ago . . .

Half remembered
Half forgot
The reedy notes
Awkward
Thin
And high.
A time ago
A time ago . . .

Dry-hot
The nascent voice
That sang
A reaching song.
Thick-eared
Elbow-edged
And ragged rhymed.
A time ago
A time ago . . .

But sweet
Oh sweet to hear
In memory's pit
The crude refrain

Tongue-torn
From album of the past.
A time ago
A time ago . . .

And could it be
That in a nap
Nostalgic head
Lends lilt
To callow tunelessness
That filled
A surging throat?
A time ago
A time ago . . .

Half remembered
Half forgot
The reedy notes
Awkward
Thin
And high.
A rhyme ago
A rhyme ago . . .

XXXVIII

And do you yearn
Old Spindleshanks
For whitehot oasthouse
In remembered Tartarus?
Where once
A fevered antic youth
Writhed nightly
With a throbbing need unslaked.

XXXIX

A poem
Comes . . .
When mindless winds
Tear off
The shingled rooftops
Of a man.

XL

Odd Pinnate

The mated leaves
Along the branch's bend
Ignore the lonely omen
At the end.

Odd′ - Pin′nate, *adj. Bot.* Pinnate with a single
terminal leaflet.

WEBSTER'S DICTIONARY

XLI

Elegy

Upon the grass
Stands plastic lamb
With flowers in its back.
Within the grave
A small child lies
Who knew three years of life,
Then left to join her elders here
Beneath the solemn pines.

And can the mother
Hear its cries
When thunder roars above
And pelting rain insensate beats
Upon that small bouquet?
Or do the ghosts from round about
Scoop up the tiny form
And rock her back to sleep again
Embraced by phantom arms?

XLII

Manor Born

Among the plants
Upon the sill
How nice to saunter
at my will.

Though stroll
Is only window-wide
I tour estate
With lordly pride!

XLIII

Invitation

Once upon a time ago,
As we are wont to say,
Will start our simple rhyme below
The real old fashioned way.

Together then, come let us fly
To some strange mythic place,
A dancing ring perchance espy
Or find some elfin trace.

See giant and witch and errant knight
And princess . . . oh, so fair,
Lovely as the Northern Lights
With dew upon her hair.

Dive deep within the jade-green seas,
There pirate treasures rest
And coral stands high as redwood trees
Wherein shy mermaids nest.

Together then, come let us fly
To where our childhood lay,
In golden land of makebelieve
Where wonders filled each day.

XLIV

Morris Blackburn — Painter
1902–1979

Paladin with brush as lance
And palette for a shield
Quick to laughter yet quick to ire
The champion of a Muse.

It mattered not at tourney's end
How went unequal joust,
But that the lists — you staunchly dared
To guard quixotic dream.

XLV

To a Note

Sweet love child of abrasion born,
When fate lay naked on the air
And bow skimmed span of tautened string.
Just then, whole destiny of man
Flew high upon a single note
To soar beyond mortality.

XLVI

Harpsichord

Filigreed echoes
Of a harpsichord
Facet time-washed crystals
Of the wakened chandelier.

Slivered Bach
In pale refracted flight
Evokes
An amber interval
Within
A sound-stirred heart.

XLVII

Irregular Ode to Mozart

The flexing notes entwining mesh
And weave a silver shawl
To drape about the shoulders
Of an evanescent shade.

Daintily
The slender flute
With trilling voice of mountain rill
Winds its way midst pizzicato strings,
To laugh and swirl upon the air,
A ferine otter frolicking.

XLVIII

*To George Rochberg**

Pavan Arcadian
Within a glade . . .
Lifted arms
To Nemorensis Rex . . .
Above, upon a depth of blue,
A wingèd riddle hangs.

Sere the past
To those in flight.
Thin the chords
To seekers of the time . . .
The lost ago . . .
Within tomorrow's sound.

*Upon hearing his *Summer Serenade*.

XLIX

I list the strings narrate a tale
In flushing voice of youth,
And hear the keys lend vivid glimpse
Of men and life agone.
I see a spectral scribe indite
A mouldering manuscript;
I marvel new at print and press
And those who resurrect.

Upon hearing Joseph de Pasquale and Vladimir
Sokoloff play the *Sonata for Viola and Piano
in E♭ major* by Allessandro Rolla, (1757–1841).

L

I sought my poem everywhere
Until I met a bee . . .
It led me where a harebell hid
Beneath a lichened tree.

LI

Plea to a Nascent Line

Frail as fledgling thrust from nest
Strange as figure in a mist
Wilful as capricious lover
Witching as some ancient tongue.

Taunt me not by disappearing
Ere your nuptials with my pen
Let me cherish you forever
Held in amber poetry.

LII

The old one isn't talking
To the air . . .
He chats with ghosts
That wait beside his chair.

LIII

Walking widdershins through life
Tasting toadstools as I pass
Brushing cobwebs from my face
Trending toward the scimitar . . .

LIV

Tabula Rasa

Erased by age,
The convolutions of his probing mind
A *tabula rasa* has become . . .
The palimpsestuous levels of his words
Now snarled as ball of yarn
By kitten paws.

Yet in his eyes a spark remains
That seems to plead for end of farce,
And begs to let the body follow on
To where the absent mind has fled.

LV

"Wait . . ."
He shouted
In the gale
"I had not finished
Quite
My tale . . ."

A sigh came rolling
From the sea
"Nor we
Nor thee
Nor those
To be . . ."

LVI

Old woman in the entryway
With claw-clutched shopping bag,
What past engulphs those rheumy eyes
That bleakly stare beyond?

A farm against blue stands of spruce,
Long distant years from here?
A kitchen redolent of stews
Abrim with aproned love?

Grim beldam in the entryway,
There is no hearthstone now
Nor bosom hug nor clattering pans
To tell of dinnertime.

Just night and offal for your bed
In grey, grey city dust.
Just footfalls of the passersby
Who see you not at all.

LVII

I hear the stern subtraction
Of the clock upon the stand
As it renders horal statements
To be paid upon demand.

LVIII

Lost Innocence

He wandered from the citadel of youth
To stand upon the tiptoes of his mind
And peer beyond the walls of ignorance.
It was a devastating sight to view
Erasing smile Boeotian evermore . . .
Lost virginal innocence beyond recall,
But in return a compensation rare,
Defying simple telling of it here.

LIX

Don't believe my face, dear friend,
The wrinkles are not true
A whitened beard and thinning hair
About me give no clue!

For hid beneath the false façade
There dwells a childlike imp.
It is a fact you must accept
Although my leg is gimp.

This pixie frolics through my days
And never will he age
'Tis really just the me out front
Who seems austere and sage!

So don't believe my face, dear friend,
For even when I die
The imp will live where Springtime sings
And leaves dance 'gainst the sky.

LX

Once . . .
Atop a lonely tor
I heard a flageolet.
And though, long past,
Pan cantered by . . .
Today, I hear it yet.

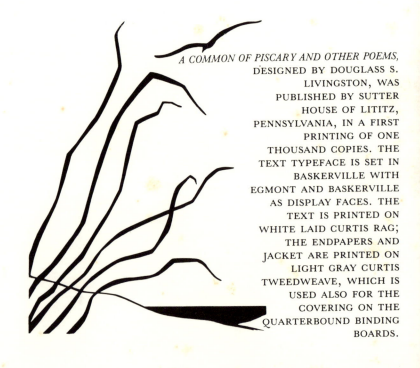

A COMMON OF PISCARY AND OTHER POEMS, DESIGNED BY DOUGLASS S. LIVINGSTON, WAS PUBLISHED BY SUTTER HOUSE OF LITITZ, PENNSYLVANIA, IN A FIRST PRINTING OF ONE THOUSAND COPIES. THE TEXT TYPEFACE IS SET IN BASKERVILLE WITH EGMONT AND BASKERVILLE AS DISPLAY FACES. THE TEXT IS PRINTED ON WHITE LAID CURTIS RAG; THE ENDPAPERS AND JACKET ARE PRINTED ON LIGHT GRAY CURTIS TWEEDWEAVE, WHICH IS USED ALSO FOR THE COVERING ON THE QUARTERBOUND BINDING BOARDS.